Other Books

The Legend of AngelGreen

TRANSMISSIONS
from the
HEARTSTAR

Angelic poetic messages of spiritual awakening...

By Glenn Volmer
(aka Ra Mikael Elohim)

DragonEye Publishing

Transmissions from the HeartStar:
Copyright 2016, By Glenn Volmer
(Pen Name - Ra Mikael Elohim)

Copyright 2016, The Glenn Volmer Copyright

All rights reserved. No part of this book may be reproduced or transmitted in any form or by any means, electronic or mechanical, including photocopying, recording, or by any information storage and retrieval system without permission in writing from the author.

First Edition
First Printing April 1, 2017
ISBN 13: 978-1-61500-143-9 (Paperback)
ISBN 13: 978-1-61500-125-5 (Epub)
ISBN 13: 978-1-61500-177-4 (PDF)

Library of Congress Control Number: 2017935700

Published by, Poetry and Spiritual Inspirational, an Imprint of
DragonEye Publishing

Publisher info.
DragonEye Publishing
753 Linden Place, Unit A
Elmira, NY 14901 USA

Publisher's website
DragonEyePublishers.com

Contact: Orders@DragonEyePublishers.com

About the Author

Glenn E. Volmer – AKA (Ra Mikael Elohim) - Heartstar, was a native of Colorado, he lived in Evergreen Colorado for several years, with his fat cat Ms. Neptune Furball. There he had enjoyed a magnificent view off his deck of Mt. Evans. As had maintains a small fleet of road racing bicycles, and way too many pairs of X-C racing skis.

In the Memory of
Glenn Elwood Volmer
9/10/1943 - 10 /20/2006

Dedication

This book is lovingly dedicated to Grace of Mt. Shasta, whose beautiful friendship has been an inspiration to me. Thank you for all you've given me, and shared with me. I thank you for opening my heart to allow love to enter. Thank you for changing my life with your love, and most of all, thank you for loving me at a time when I wasn't doing a very good job of loving myself. Beloved Grace. Angel of The Lilies, I simply love you, but you know that. See you on the Ship...

Blessed out in the arms of Grace at the Star-Borne Angelic reunion,
Snowmass, Colorado, June 1991

Table of Contents

1 Foreword

3 Ancient Sentinels of the Mountains
4 The Heart of God
5 Listen With Your Heart
6 Beloved Grace
8 Sister Rita
9 The Way-Showers
11 Mother Terra
13 Heartlove
15 Starlight Dancer
17 Love is
19 The Light From Above
20 The Silence of the Stars
22 God's Playground
23 O'child of The Stars
24 The Great Awakening
25 In The Arms of Grace
26 Ascension
27 It is Time
28 How Shall I know You?
29 Destiny With The Stars
30 In The Stillness
31 Angel from the Future
32 The Messenger
33 A Touch Upon Your Face
34 The Winds of Change
35 Messages From The Second Stargate
36 Mountain Spring

37 Dear Sweet Jeanne
38 The Changing Tides of Time
39 The Rainbow Ships
40 Rainbow Beamships
41 You are my heart
43 Vision
44 Afterword

46 Acknowledgments

Foreword

These messages (transmissions) are about stories of awakening. When I first heard of 11:11, I was very drawn to it, though I didn't know why. In May of 1991, I met Solara in Denver, Colorado, which lead me to attend the Star-borne Angelic reunion in June of 1991 in Snowmass, Colorado. During this week turned out to be the most intense and profound week of my entire life.

It was there I met Grace (of Mt. Shasta) and her gentleness and love changed my life forever. I became very active in 11:11 activities, and participated with larger groups in Denver on the actual day (Jan. 11, 1992). Since meeting Solara, my spiritual growth has accelerated at a rate I found astonishing. I never imagined or dreamed I would be writing poetry. There is a mountain in Colorado called Mt. Evans, which features America's highest paved highway to 14,264 feet. On that mountain live a small group of ancient (2,000 -2,500 years old) Bristle cone pine trees. I've been very aware of the wonderful energy up there for years, and that is where my poetry writing begins. The first poem (Ancient Sentinels of the Mountain) was written about those lovely old trees. They continue to nature me and bless me with their love and wisdom.

I find that I am quite sensitive to Angelic energy, and can sense it in other people. Many of the poems are written about special people in my life who have deeply touched my heart. As the awakening process continues for me, I know I shall continue to put my feelings into my poetry, for I see their purpose is to function as triggers for people to help them awaken to their true spiritual nature.

We are spiritual beings having a human experience. With virtually every poem or transmission, there is a story behind it. I would be honored to share that with any reader. Archangel Mikael has been the source behind several transmissions (poems). I hope that at least one or more of these writings touches your heart in a special way, and provides a catalyst for your own spiritual growth and awakening. In love and light, dear ones, I remain truly yours in service to the ONE. Blessing be... May your hearts always be in the arms of Grace?

Ra Mikael Elohim Heartstar

Ancient Sentinels of the Mountains

An Angel gently, softly, walks amongst you,
weeping with joy,
at your loving message.
Home, Home, Home...
Yes. I know, gentle ones,
I know...
How long you have waited for the doorway to open.
When the Angels turned the key,
you were, at last set free
to return to your celestial home
among the stars.
Long have I heard your message of love
whispered through the endless corridors of
timeless time;
gently carried upon the cosmic winds
to my heart.
Home, Home, Home...
Yes, dear gentle ancient ones,
I know...
The immense magnitude of your all-encompassing love.
It touches me deeply, and fills my heart
with peace, gentleness, harmony, and great joy.
I feel your nurturing presence
healing the old hurts in my soul
as your gentle love embraces my heart.
I weep openly, as your love
washes away my pain,
and we melt,
into a blessed Oneness...

The Heart of God

Embraced by the cloudy mists,
I feel so nurtured and loved
by a greater Presence...
Oh, the love I feel,
it takes me home, it takes me home...
I'm enveloped in a sea of intense gentleness,
the mist feels like gentle Angel wings
lovingly holding me,
close, to the heart of God.
Mikael, Mikael and the legions...
My Angelic brethren fill
my heart with joy...
I surrender myself to your love.
There's a serenity sweeping over me
like the gentle mists that now surround me.
I release myself to your tender caress...
Peace, Peace, Peace...
Oh beloved mountains,
my heart opens to your sweet love, we truly are One...

Listen With Your Heart

Be still, my child
be still...
Listen with your heart.
I breathe deep
and release myself to a Greater Presence...
I feel cradled by a loving force
so strong, yet so gentle.
It's the love of God...
A nurturing presence,
yet, what I sense
is not separate from who I AM...
I am awakening...
My heart fills with the I AM essence
in the gentle stirring
of the cosmic winds
that caresses my soul so sweetly...
And I realize, I AM,
what, I've been longing for...
Be Still, my child
listen with your heart...
Be at peace,
for God's plan,
is unfolding perfectly...
Be the Love You Are...

Beloved Grace

Beautiful, Beautiful
Angel of the lilies
Heart of my Heart...
YOU, opened the door for me
to see...
Not with my eyes,
but with my heart.
YOU, held me so close
and let my tears
wash away,
all those ancient fears...
YOU, opened the door
to let me receive,
instead of to always give.
YOU, gave to me
the greatest gift of love,
I've ever known...
YOU, opened the door
for me,
to really be able to see - ME...
Such a gift...
Angel of the lilies
Heart of my Heart,
Meeting you,
truly, has been
the most significant event
of my entire life.
YOU hold my life in your arms,
YOU hold my heart in your life...
And I,

Transmissions from the HeartStar

simply,
Love you, with all my heart...

Sister Rita

Dearest One,
Star child of the universe...
YOU truly are an Angel,
though you don't it...
Your gentle, innocent heart
touches me deeply...
Awaken, my child
to who you truly are.
For you are an Angel,
though you don't know it.
I see an Angel
looking back at me,
when I gaze into your eyes.
YOU are Light and Love,
and the Spirit of God
breathed into form...
Now is the time of the Great Awakening,
Precious One,
Now is the time to fulfill our Divine Mission
on planet Earth,
and why we chose to come here now.
Your longing and tender sadness
touches me,
ever so sweetly.
For your gentle, innocent heart
is so full of love...
Awaken Dearest child
for you truly are an Angel
from the stars...
Beloved One, it's time to come home...

The Way-Showers

Long have I traveled,
through innumerable incarnations
mired in the sands of time,
Bound in the harness of forgetfulness.
Onward, ever onward have I struggled
encased in a dimension of such density
that ever I forgot my purpose, my divine mission...
Yet, something inside me kept whispering, HOME,
HOME...
Long have I traveled on a path of darkness, sleeping,
yet thy Father's hand has always been guiding me,
ever when I knew it not.
A flicker of light called faith
has been my beacon to follow,
through eons of the illusion we call time.
Yet always, has there been a deep yearning
to return to the stars, to the light, the One.
Now, my earthly harness of forgetfulness is dissolving
as I awaken from my long, long slumber.
I am awakening to see that, I AM the Light
I've been following home to thy Father's heart.

I finally see the reason I'm here...
And the reason is called love.
I see I AM a beacon for others to follow.
Awaken, my starry brethren
for the Doorway is at long-last-OPEN.
It's time to go home to the LIGHT...
We are the Way-Showers...
Cast off your old tattered garments of doubt and fear

for they no longer serve you.
Long have you forgotten you are a child of the stars...
Embrace, with joy, your new robes of LIGHT, my children.
Do you still doubt your worthiness to wear such a robe?
Remember, your heart is forever embraced in the arms of GRACE,
and when you have forgotten who you truly are, simply ask yourself;
Does one flower deserve the sun more than another?
Awaken to the magnificence of who you are
and why you came here to serve...
Look within your heart for the answers you seek,
for within your heart is the LIGHT of God's Love.
And that love is why we are here.
We truly are the Way-Showers...
It's time to go home... To the LIGHT
of the ONE...

Mother Terra

Rain Rain Rain...
Oh yes, Mother Earth,
I feel your love
pouring from heaven,
Your message caresses my heart...
Cleanse, Purify, Nurture,
Cleanse, Purify, Nurture...
I breathe your loving essence
into my soul,
I feel your healing
and I weep with joy...
Oh, Mother Earth,
Your gentleness rains down
in sweet, loving abundance,
to touch my simple heart
with your love...
Yes, You are changing too,
I feel it, I sense it...
The rain nurtures me with
your love, enveloping my heart,
washing away my old hurts
with your tears from heaven...
Sweet Mother Earth
I feel your loving presence
permeate the very core of
who I AM...
I feel your boundless love
for your children...
I feel your message in every raindrop,
Cleansing, purifying, and nurturing...

Your message is love,
Love is why we are here.
The air is so sweet
with the fragrance of your rain,
and in that sweetness,
I feel the eternal love
of the God, Goddess,
All that Is...
Peace, my child of the stars,
All is well
for you are surrounded
with love...

Heartlove

I feel so much love
pouring through me
like an eternal tide
washing upon the shores of time.
I am awakening
to a greater awareness
of the ALL that is.
I AM seeing a glimpse
of who I truly am,
and it overpowers my heart
with feeling of love,
with a joy so boundless
I feel unable to express it...
It's the Father God and
the Mother Earth
awakening the children of the stars...
Cast off the covers from your eyes
and see just who you truly are...
God's Love, animated in fields of matter
reflecting His Love in an infinite, endless
array of expression...
I AM
an expression of that Love...
I see it's the force
behind the form...
Life, beautiful, glorious life...
God's infinite Love
reflected in countless expressions
of the ONE...
My heart is bursting with love,

overflowing like a living, starry Mandela
of awareness...
Spreading light into the world,
like a flower petal, opening deeper
and deeper unto itself...
Growing, awakening, becoming, changing,
radiating, glowing, shining.
Being... Simply Being...
The cosmic consciousness of love,
incarnate, I AM.
An Angel, dancing in biological clay,
feeling the stardust coursing
through my veins,
like shooting stars
from the heart of the ONE...
Feeling the pulse of the Universe
with every beat of my own heart,
Yearning, longing, to return home,
to the stars...

Starlight Dancer

OH Beautiful Precious Angel,
How you touch my heart...
Being with you brings such sweet,
simple joy to me...
Your eyes, OH GOD, your eyes...
I see star systems, galaxies of light, sparkling,
dancing, in your eyes...
The radiance of the cosmos flashing,
dancing, playing, being, reflecting your
inner beauty for all the worlds of God's infinite
creation to see... In your eyes...
When I hold you in my arms,
I feel... OH GOD, I feel... YOU,
I feel each others essence, merging,
melting, dissolving into a blessed state of oneness,
of serenity, calmness, joy, love harmony
peace, trust, beauty, innocence, bliss...
OH so sweet...
And I realize that what I feel
from you, is simply a mirror of my own heart.
The love we feel, simply a mirror
of God's infinite love...
I'm so deeply moved
by your innocent heart...
Telling you I Love You,
is so easy,
for how could I not love you,
a beautiful, golden Angel,
a radiant beam of light
dancing with joy

Transmissions from the HeartStar

upon the starwaves
of my heart...

Love Is...

A pinpoint of LIGHT
penetrating the darkness of duality,
A shimmering beacon in the fog shrouded
ocean of third dimensional density...
A pinpoint of LIGHT to guide
a world longing to return
to its celestial home among the stars.
Tiny, flickering, pulsating, yet growing... Brighter...
A pinpoint of LIGHT...
a beacon of awareness
piercing the veils of forgetfulness...
Light, Love, Joy unfolding,
blooming into a vast
cosmic consciousness,
of the essence of God...

A pinpoint of LIGHT
growing into a wave
of expanding, all encompassing love,
sweeping away the dust of eons
of unawareness, slumber and illusion...
A wave of Light beaming forth
from five billion hearts beating as ONE,
cascading over the shores of darkness,
dissolving all sand castles of illusion in its path.
Awaken my starry children
to who you truly are...

Transmissions from the HeartStar

We are now living the destiny
we have prophesied for ourselves...

Awaken Light Beings.
Illuminate our beloved Terra
with the Light and Love,
from within your hearts...
Transform our precious home into
the shining jewel of the cosmos
she was destined to be...
A pinpoint of Light,
becoming a tidal wave of Love,
flooding our lives with the I AM Presence...

Awaken children of the stars,
let your light shine forth into a
world crying for your love.
Now is the time of the Great Awakening...
Rub the sleep of the ages from your eyes
my children, and simply Be
the shining beacon of Love
you came here
To Be,
In ONENESS.

The Light from above

Children of the stars
CAN'T YOU FEEL IT!
How can you not be aware
of the love?!
It's growing, OH GOD, it's growing,
manifesting in countless hearts
of the children of Light,
flooding beloved Terra with
God's loving presence...
Home, we're going home,
Home to thy Father's heart,
Home to the Light
that lives in each of us.
CAN'T YOU FEEL IT!
Awaken my starry brethren,
our family of AN...
Slumber no longer under
the covers of duality and illusion,
Cast them aside, rise up
and dance in the Light of remembrance!
O'children of the stars
awaken, dear precious ones
listen to your heart
for within lies the answers you seek...
The Light from above truly
radiates from within the heart...

The Silence of the Stars

The silence of the stars
fills me with awe,
and touches my heart deeply
with the vastness of the cosmos...
How my heart dances with delight
with each meteor I see
streaking across the heavens...
And I feel their message,
alive, we are alive!
The universe is teeming with life,
with boundless love and ecstasy...
I sense such a closeness to the stars
for I know I'm part of them.
Every meteor is a flash of
God's essence, illuminating the night sky
with loving, radiant stardust...
Oh God. I feel so alive and vibrant.
There is such an overwhelming desire
in my heart, to merge,
back with the starry realms
from whence I came,
so long ago...
Gazing deep into the night sky
I begin to weep with such
a tender yearning...
I feel the stars calling me,
pulling me, like the moon
moves the tides...
I feel the eternalness of my soul
pulsating with the twinkling of the stars

as they gently sing to me...
Awaken o'child of the stars,
it is the dawn of a new awareness
for Mother Earth,
and her beloved star children...
Awaken and feel,
the silence of the stars...

GOD'S Playground
(Mt. Evans - Colorado)

The brutal beauty of the high mountains
fills me with a deep sense of awe...
It's the power of Nature
in the biting wind and stinging snow,
yet I feel such a quiet tranquility
settling over me,
as the grandeur of this landscape
presents such a harsh beauty to behold...
I sense a powerful gentleness at work here,
and my simple heart
feels the hand of a Greater Presence,
manifesting, creating this immense beauty.
There's a consciousness here of the Highest Essence,
the deepest purity, a state of timeless Isness...
God's playground, covered in swirling clouds of snow,
moved by the cosmic winds that have
shaped and sculptured universes with the power of love.
For all this incredible beauty is
truly a creation of love...
It's that love I feel so deeply
which brings me again and again,
to the high mountains,
for they are part of
the Holy Essence of
who
I AM...

O'Child of the Stars

Come journey with me my child,
for we return to the stars...
Your dear heart is filled with such tender gentleness
yet is burdened by sadness and heaviness;
come journey with me my child,
we shall play with the Angels,
and dance amongst the starbeams...
Awaken, angel of Light, to who you truly are.
I feel your longing to return home.
I sense it in you so much,
for I share the same desire with you...
Now is the time to let go of the past,
and step into the radiance of Love's vibration.
Listen to your heart, precious one,
for withing lies the way home, it is HOME...
Trust who you are, my dear, for who you are,
is gentleness, joy, laughter, Light and Love;
Open your heart to let the boundless love
of God come flooding in...
Spread your Angelic Wings of Light,
and come fly with me, o'child of the stars,
as we return back to the very essence
of who we truly are...
Now is the time to give your love to someone
very special... yourself...
And touch the heart of God that dwells within...

The Great Awakening

The time is running out, my children,
the illusion we've struggled under
for eons is ending.
Time as we know it, is of the essence,
for very soon there will be
monumental choices to be made.
The season of great awakening
is upon us, Dear Ones.
The answers to what choices we
make are all found within our hearts.
The family of light is emerging from
its cocoon of darkness it has
been encumbered with for countless eons.
Now the shimmering butterfly of love
can, at long last, spread its luminous, gossamer
wings of light and fly freely once more,
for our time has come
to return home to the stars...

In The Arms of Grace

It's Love Isn't It!
That's why we are here...
It's Love...
Embracing us, in the arms of Grace,
holding us in the heart of God...
It's Love Isn't It?
That's what has kept us going
through all these eons of time...
Yes, I see it now,
It's so clear to me...
It's Love...
It was for love, when we made
our choice to serve here,
and it's that love, that
draws us Home again...
Our vast starry family is reuniting
for the journey homeward...
For as we travel our celestial path,
always are we lovingly cradled,
gently, oh so gently, so sweetly held
In the arms of GRACE...

Ascension

Weep no tears for me, my child
except tears of joy...
For although I have gone,
I have not left you...
Love knows not the boundaries of time nor space...
When you gaze at the stars late at night
and you feel, sense, a presence...
An essence stirring your soul...
It is I, my child,
sending you waves of love
from my heart to yours,
across the vast, cosmic starfields...
When you are very still,
listen closely as I whisper
words of universal love,
deep into your divine consciousness...
I AM here, o'child of Light,
whispering; awaken, awaken,
precious one...
Beckoning you to follow your heart
back to the stars...

It is Time

It Is TIME,
children of the stars
to come home...
It is time to awaken
from your ancient slumber...
It is time to be who you truly are.
Reach out across the cosmos,
and touch the hearts of your long lost family.
You will touch them with your love,
for your loving vibration
is resonating in
the fields of densest matter...
And you will touch other hearts
with your angelic presence,
radiating, beaming waves of love,
seeking hearts that are open to receiving
your starry vibrations.
For love is
the language of the cosmos...
Love is the reason
we came here...
Love is the reason
it is time,
we shall return to our starry home...

How Shall I Know You?

How shall I know you, my child?
I shall know you
by your starry essence...
by the love vibration
you gently send out from your heart.
I shall know you
by the starlight captured in your angel eyes,
by the radiance beaming forth
from your spirit of Oneness
with the God, Goddess All That Is...
I shall know you, precious one
by your sweet, tender gentleness
that feels so familiar to me.
For you see, my luminous angel,
we have been together before...
Galaxies of light were our playgrounds then,
a macrocosm of star systems we called Home,
for we truly were children of the stars;
dancing, laughing with playful, gleeful abandon...
We were living madalas of shimmering starlight
radiating our vibrant love
through the stargates of timeless time...
Portals of many dimensions did we know,
And I shall know you, beautiful Angel,
by the reflection
of me,
I see in you...

Destiny with the Stars

Dear Ones
I soon shall be gone,
for it is time to fulfill my destiny.
Through eons of time have I traveled,
just to be with you in this lifetime.
This is the one I've been waiting for
and my earthly mission is nearing completion.
But fear not, precious ones,
for I shall return to be with you,
to help remove the veil that separates us
My heart is so full of joy
for I know I'm going Home,
and my joy is your joy, Dear ones.
Although dimensions separate us
our hearts beat as one.
Come travel with me, through the stargates
to beyond the beyond.
Wake up o'sleepy children of the stars,
and see who you truly are.
Dear ones, I soon shall be gone,
the first wave is about to leave
and I will be joining them.
Yet I remain only a thought wave away.
Changes are coming, Dear Ones
and I shall appear to you
when you least expect it, to remind you,
of Your destiny with the stars...

In the Stillness

It's still, so still here...
In the stillness lies the answers you seek.
In the stillness, you can hear
the pulse of the cosmic consciousness
reverberating with the synchronicity
of your own eternal essence...
In the stillness, you know you are not alone
for the Angelic Realms are always with you.
You sense a presence; All-Knowing, All-Loving...
The I AM consciousness,
and you realize you are part of a greater wholeness,
An omniscience of the deepest magnitude,
the Highest Order, an Eternal Divinity...
You know you have come from the Light, to serve during
these times of great need,
and you know, unto the Light you shall return.
Long has been your journey
through eons of illusion and darkness,
yet now you see you really never
left the path of Light.
In the stillness, your heart feels
a deepening sense of overpowering joy,
for you truly know
that soon you will
be going Home,
to the stars...

Angel from the Future

Oh Starchild, starbright,
I have seen the future tonight...
Your starry radiance beams
forth from your sweet, innocent heart...
I sense in you
our tomorrow's,
here today...
How you sparkle, glow and shine...
A purest drop of angelic essence
dancing your way into our hearts
with your laughter.
I have seen the future tonight,
and it's love!
Alive, pulsating, vibrating to the new energies
from the other side of the doorway.
The life force of the stars
sparkles in your eyes...
O' little angel from the future,
how you have captured my heart.
I feel your higher vibration,
I sense a difference in you,
for what I feel is also a reflection of me...
I have seen the future tonight,
and it is of
the Purest Light...

The Messenger

I AM a messenger of love
sent from the starry realms of LIGHT.

I AM a beacon of love shining through
the darkness of illusion and duality
to transform our planet,
to fulfill our destiny of being
the I AM presence
in living manifestation.

I fully accept who I AM.

I claim the power and the Love I Am.

I AM a way-shower.

I AM awakening.

I AM,

LOVE...

A touch upon your face

A touch upon your face,
as I brush the hair from your eyes...
A touch upon your face...
All the love I AM,
flowing through one finger,
gently, oh so gently...
A touch upon your face, my love.
The love of the cosmos
whispered, without a word,
but with a touch...
A touch upon your face,
for touching you
is touching the face of God.
You close your eyes
to receive all my gentle love,
and I weep, for I know
who you are is truly part of me...
And I feel your love so deeply,
for are we not each reflections of God's infinite love.
Universes, galaxies, of love and light
beyond the beyond,
All this I feel, with simply,
a touch upon your face, my love...
Touching the deepest essence of
Who I AM,
with
a touch upon your face...

The Winds of Change

The winds of change are upon us my children
lifting the veils of illusion from our eyes.
Can you not feel the changes in your heart,
for the quantum awakening of mankind
is just over the horizon,
the greater reality awaits us all,
for the experiment of duality and separateness
has played itself out.
The time of completion of human history
is truly at hand.
Awaken, O'Children of Light
to see, just who you really are...
Beautiful angelic spirits serving the One,
in animated forms of matter...
The winds of change are upon us,
beckoning us to open our hearts
to the waves of energy and love,
pouring into our lives
from the celestial realms of
the I AM presence.
We are truly on
our homeward journey...
Unfurl your wings of Golden Light,
my Children of the Stars,
for our cosmic family is eagerly
awaiting our return Home...

Messages from the Second Stargate

On gossamer beams of light
they come,
dancing their way into our hearts...
Messages of love from beyond the beyond,
beckoning us to awaken from
our eons of slumber, under
dense blankets of illusion.
Rays of the purest light
shimmering with th
promise of new tomorrows.
The dawn of a new consciousness
is upon us
and its message is simply...
LOVE...
Innocence and trusting
sparkles like
gleaming crystals on the sands of time.
Come children of the stars,
open your heart to bask
in the joy of the Creator's
boundless love.
For on gossamer beams of light, the come
waves of love, cascading upon
the shores of our hearts,
to change our lives, and to
remind us our eternalness
as luminous beings of Light...

Mountain Spring

It's spring in my beloved mountains,
and I weep with joy at such beauty...
My heart is so deeply touched by
the loving presence of God's
hand at work...
It's so wonderful to be alive and
feel this wonder... this joy...
My heart is full of love
my heart is home in my mountains.
For I know I am part
of this magnificent expression of love.
The very essence of who I Am
simply merges with the
love... OH the Love...
I feel
in the spring
in my beloved mountains.

Dear Sweet Jeanne

Oh innocent child of the stars,
don't you see it's time
to wake up to who you truly are...
You are lightness and purity
and innocence and trusting...
See how the stones and crystals
call out to you...
Awaken dear heart
for your angelic essence
touches the realms of higher dimensions.
Your innocent heart
touches me deeply, and I
share your joy as your
heart feels the secrets
of the stones.
You see with your heart
precious child, now awaken
to the destiny you've chosen,
and allow yourself to
simply be, the
beautiful angel
you truly are...

The changing tides of Time

Changes are coming
my children,
changes are coming
for our beloved Mother
is casting off the shackles of density
that have bound her for eons and eons.
Our Earth is shifting dimensions
as is her family of Light Beings
manifesting the changing tides of time.
For Mother Earth mirrors her children
and the sweeping changes but reflect
the changes in our own hearts...
We are manifesting our Light Bodies
as we change and grow and leave behind
the old ways that no longer serve us
like old garments that no longer fit.
For we are awakening to see that
we are truly children of the stars.
We are awakening to our Divine heritage
as we remember from whence we came
so long, long, ago.
Changes are coming, my children,
look deep within,
for they all begin in the heart...

The Rainbow Ship

Oh, Rainbow ship of clouds,
I stand here awestruck at your beauty;
shimmering, shifting, translucent rainbow hues
in the clouds right above me... it's a Lightship!
I know I caught you changing dimensions
in the clouds,
where people look, but they <u>do</u> <u>not</u> <u>SEE</u>
I feel your energy, your love, your light.
Your celestial presence
touches my simple heart... deeply...
I sense you wanted me to see you,
a rainbow reminder of our own divinity.
I feel the veils being lifted
as the I AM presence
manifests to the children of the Stars.
A rainbow message of love
among the clouds,
to touch the very essence of my soul
with your love...

Rainbow Beamships

On Beams of Rainbow Light
you travel, magnificent Beamships
from the Great Central Sun.
You journey here to touch my heart, my soul...
Watching you in the sky,
fills the very essence of who I Am
with anticipation, with excitement, with longing,
with a knowing,
we are not alone.
I sense a cosmic oneness
with the Brotherhood of Light,
who travel on beams of Rainbows
through the stargates,
from Beyond the great Beyond.
Waves upon waves
of Rainbow love fill the skies
with a presence so vast in scope
my heart dances with joy
at your message,
HOME Beloved ones,
it's time to come
HOME...

You are my Heart

My love, my love, my love,
there's an entire universe in your arms.
As you hold me close, I shut my eyes to see,
light, swirling clouds, luminous galaxies
stretching into infinity.
Love, so much love I feel, I beging to cry and cry,
I feel so safe in your arms.
The old hurts are dissolving in my tears,
wave after wave of old pain being released,
healed... gone...
I feel your soft hair against my cheek,
I'm aware we are no longer separate,
our hearts beat as One, You and I
merge into a state of blessed Oneness, Beingness,
Isness...
A single entity of the purest Light and Love...
There's an entire universe in your arms, my love,
my love...
I see us flying, floating through the stars,
oh, the colors...
I feel so warm, so loved, and realize
you're holding me not only with your arms
but have embraced me with your translucent
wing of love...
I open my eyes to look at you,
and I blink in amazement, for I'm seeing myself!
You, my love, are my mirror, my reflection of
my soul...
The love and gentleness I'm so attracted to in
you,

is simply a reflection of myself I see in you.
Oh, my love, my love, my love,
now, I understand your meaning
when you tell me, you'll always be with me,
we'll always be together,
for our hearts truly are One,
you are my heart,
my love, my love, my love...

Vision

Dearest One,
you are a celebration of Life.
In your deep, sparkling eyes
is truly the Light of the I AM presence
manifested in glorious form...
How your sweet innocence touches my heart.
You are a ray of God's love, lighting
up the worlds of all those you touch.
You are a celebration of Life,
I feel your starry, angelic vibrations,
and I'm so moved to know who you are...
A lovely Angel of Light,
beaming your way into our hearts
with your smile, your laugh,
your very presence...
You are a vision
of the future,
here now, to bless our lives,
just by simply being
the love you are...

Afterword

I cannot think of a more fitting end to this volume than to leave you with one of my favorite poems from Graces' book of poetry. Meeting Grace years ago has continued to be the most significant event of my entire life. She triggered an awakening in me that is ongoing to this day. For those of you fortunate enough to have ever met her, had a healing session wither, or simply, have gently hugged her, you know what I mean. Precious Angel of the Lilies, Heart of my heart, I simply Love you. Namaste.

From Grace

And you are beautiful
And you touched the earth so sweetly
Did you not?
You gave of an essence
Know only to the Angels
And to the stars.
And little did you know
How you blessed the earth
Where you passed…

(A Language of Light copyrighted, Grace, P.O. Box1396, Mt. Shasta, CA. 96067)

Acknowledgements

This is to acknowledge my beautiful family of 11:11 Angels, for each of you have touched my heart deeply. Thanks and Love to:

Solara, for your vision and dedication.
Matisha, my Angel Brother, for your music and goofball humor.
Elara, for your smile that melts my heart.
Elariul, for your outrageous laugh.
Alarielle, the littlest angel, with the biggest heart.
Asara, my soulmate.
Shalomar, for your patience.
Mika-Alla, for your gentleness.
Aleria, my 3-D sister, for sharing this journey with me.
Arla, wing activator, first class.
Alera, for being there for me.
Xiera, for your hugs.
Luna, what a beamer!
Wondra, for your Angel eyes.
Sara and Jeanne, for your innocence.
Paul, the reluctant angel.
Light, for lighting up my life.
Marina, for the Golden Ray of light you truly are.

And to so many, many more I wish you all my love, and may your lives be filled with grace.

Transmissions from the HeartStar

Transmissions from the HeartStar

www.ingramcontent.com/pod-product-compliance
Lightning Source LLC
Chambersburg PA
CBHW050045080526
44586CB00014B/1473